Jobs in
SUSTAINABLE
ENERGY

ROSEN
PUBLISHING®
New York

CORONA BREZINA

Published in 2010 by The Rosen Publishing Group, Inc.
29 East 21st Street, New York, NY 10010

Library of Congress Cataloging-in-Publication Data

Brezina, Corona.
Jobs in sustainable energy / Corona Brezina.—1st ed.
   p. cm.—(Green careers)
Includes bibliographical references and index.
ISBN 978-1-4358-3569-6 (library binding)
1. Renewable energy sources—Vocational guidance—Juvenile
literature. I. Title.
TJ808.B74 2010
621.042023—dc22

                                                            2009021855

Manufactured in Malaysia
CPSIA Compliance Information: Batch #TW10YA: For Further Information contact Rosen Publishing, New York,
New York at 1-800-237-9932

On the cover: A wind turbine.

On the title page: Left: A scientist analyzes a sample of algae.
Right: Workers install solar panels on a rooftop.

CONTENTS

Introduction

The United States is undergoing a green transformation. The government is backing green initiatives with tax credits, grants, and expanded research into sustainable energy. States and cities are launching green initiatives. Corporations are taking steps to reduce their environmental impact. More and more consumers are choosing environmentally friendly products and considering ways they can help the environment in their daily lives.

Behind this green revolution is the realization that Americans' lifestyles—specifically, Americans' huge energy consumption—could lead to dire long-term consequences. Most of the energy used in the United States is produced

from fossil fuels. People use electricity generated by coal power plants, drive cars fuelled by gasoline, and heat their homes with natural gas. All of these fossil fuels release carbon dioxide into the atmosphere. Increasing levels of atmospheric carbon dioxide are leading to climate change, which will impact the entire world.

Over half of the oil used in the United States is imported. This means that much of the money spent on oil supports the economies of other countries. Energy derived from renewable resources, such as solar and wind power, on the other hand, supports local economies. Domestically produced green energy also creates local jobs.

Currently, electricity derived from renewable resources is more expensive to produce than energy generated by fossil fuels. However, research and new innovations are lowering the cost of renewable energy. While fossil fuels might be cheaper to produce at the present time, they have significant hidden costs. Besides contributing to climate change, fossil fuels pollute and degrade the air, land, and water. These pollutants can cause serious health problems and increase the costs of health care.

Environmentally sustainable energy sources are those that can be used in such a way that the needs of the future will be met, as well as the needs of the present. Fossil fuels are not environmentally sustainable because they will eventually be depleted, though that could take centuries. Green energy sources represent environmentally sustainable alternatives to fossil fuels.

For millions of workers, the growth of sustainable energy opens up exciting career opportunities. The green energy industry is expected to expand, and it will create jobs in a huge variety of career fields. Direct jobs will include engineers, scientists, technicians, manufacturers, and installers, but there will also be a need for workers such as energy auditors, accountants, office managers, and sales representatives. In addition, many sectors of green energy, such as biomass energy and lithium-ion batteries for automobiles, are still in development. Once these technologies are ready for the market, they will provide even more jobs. Renewable energy development will continue to expand and evolve in the coming years and decades, providing a wealth of opportunities for green-collar job seekers.

Chapter One

Solar Energy

Every day, an incredible amount of renewable, non-polluting energy reaches the earth in the form of sunlight. If one hour's worth of solar energy were completely converted into usable forms, it would meet the energy needs of the entire world population for a year. If just twenty days' worth of solar radiation were completely converted into usable forms, it would equal all of the earth's energy stored in fossil fuels, including coal, oil, and natural gas.

These rows of huge solar troughs are part of a solar thermal system that makes up the 1,600-acre (647 hectares) "solar field" at the Solar Electric Generating Systems (SEGS) facility in Kramer Junction, California.

Today, solar energy provides less than 1 percent of the electricity generated in the U.S. power grid. Nevertheless, the use of solar energy grew 45 percent annually between 2000 and 2007, and it is expected to continue to grow.

The sun's energy can be converted into electricity through two different methods. Photovoltaic (PV) cells, used in rooftop solar panels, are made out of a semiconductor material, such as silicon. Sunlight that strikes the PV cells produces an electric current, and this current is channeled into an electrical circuit connected to the solar panel. Another means of using solar energy, a solar thermal system, collects sunlight as heat and uses this heat to produce electricity. A type of collector called a parabolic trough heats a fluid running through the trough that, in turn, heats steam. The steam is used to turn a turbine in a power generator.

Most current solar energy systems are small in scale, such as a few solar panels installed on the roof of a house. However, solar energy projects are becoming more ambitious. In Kramer Junction, California, nine huge plants called Solar Energy Generating Systems (SEGS) make up the largest solar energy power station in the world. The installation uses parabolic troughs to collect solar energy.

The primary drawback to solar energy lies in the availability of sunlight. In the United States, the Southwest receives the most intense solar radiation. The amount of available sunlight in other regions varies depending on factors such as the length of the day, cloud cover, and seasonal variations.

Solar energy is an expanding field, and it is expected to create new jobs for workers with an extremely wide range of backgrounds. Highly educated scientists, engineers, and researchers will make breakthroughs in collecting and using solar energy. Skilled technicians and other workers will be needed for the manufacture, installation, and maintenance of solar energy systems. Nontechnical workers will be needed to handle the business and administrative side of solar energy, ranging from marketing to investing.

Jobs in Research and Development

Solar energy is a growing field that welcomes innovation and technological advancement. Advances in solar energy begin with scientific research. This research is directed at improving existing technologies and solving problems in solar energy production. The results of this research are used to develop a commercially viable prototype, which is then tested and modified. If the results are deemed a success, the next step may be to manufacture the product on a large scale and market it. One disadvantage to current technology is that solar power systems are very expensive. Solar power systems of the future will likely be more affordable.

The National Renewable Energy Laboratory (NREL) is a renewable energy research facility supported by the U.S. Department of Energy. The lab's research areas include many projects related to solar energy. A building-integrated PV project works to incorporate PV panels into windows, roofing, and other construction materials. The

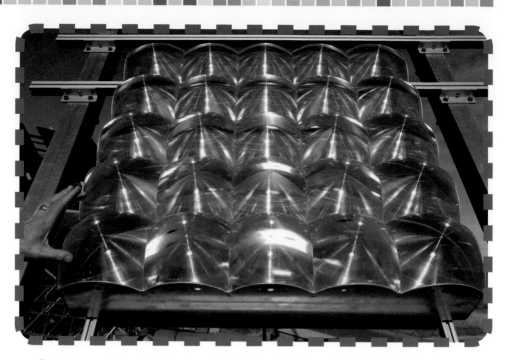

Scientists and technicians at the National Renewable Energy Laboratory (NREL) test concentrators that magnify sunlight onto solar cells. If this technology proves a success, it may be commercially developed.

High-Performance Photovoltaic initiative aims to improve the efficiency of PV cells by increasing the amount of solar radiation that is converted into electricity. Other research areas include energy storage, solar power plant technology, and the development of new materials for the construction of solar cells. NREL is just one facility—further research is being carried out in universities, government agencies, and private companies across the country.

Researchers in solar energy are highly educated in their areas of expertise. NREL employs scientists, engineers, analysts, managers, project leaders, technicians, and administrators, as well as workers in nontechnical positions. Most entry-level positions require at least a four-year degree in a field such as engineering, science, mathematics, or computer science. Many researchers hold advanced degrees such as a master's degree or a Ph.D. NREL and many other research institutions also offer internships for college students, as well as post-doctoral research positions for recent Ph.D. recipients. Such positions can provide younger researchers with a great opportunity to gain valuable experience in the field of solar energy.

Engineering the Future

Solar energy development—or any type of large-scale energy project—would not be possible without the work of engineers. Engineers apply scientific and mathematical principles to practical situations. Thanks to engineers, we live in a world with skyscrapers, interstate highways, a space program, and electronic devices ranging from air conditioners to iPods. Today, development of renewable energy sources is an exciting area in engineering with good prospects for job growth.

There are dozens of different branches of engineering, many of which can be applied to renewable energy. Mechanical engineering is one of these branches. It involves the machines that convert energy sources into usable forms, and the processes by which they do so. Mechanical engineers are involved in the research, development, design, and refinement of projects from entire power plants to automobiles and PV cells. Some

This NREL researcher tests inexpensive plastic PV cells in a lab. PV cells such as these may make solar energy more affordable for the general population.

universities offer a solar engineering specialization within their mechanical engineering programs.

Electric and electronics engineers are also in high demand in renewable energy development. Electric engineers work with equipment that transmits large amounts of electricity. Electronics engineers specialize in developing equipment, such as computers and communication systems, which use smaller amounts of power. Both of these specializations are needed in solar energy.

Chemical and materials engineers also work in the field of solar energy. Chemical engineers apply the principles of chemistry to the production and application of chemicals. Materials engineers work with the basic materials used to make products, such as plastics and semiconductors. They often study and manipulate materials at an atomic level. In the field of solar energy, materials engineers work on projects such as the development of cheaper, more efficient PV cells made out of new semiconductor materials.

First Solar

First Solar is the world's largest solar energy company that manufactures thin-film photovoltaic solar modules. First Solar's cadmium-telluride panels are more versatile and much cheaper to produce than silicon-based cells. Silicon-based cells are less efficient at converting solar energy into electricity. In 2008, First Solar became the first solar energy company to produce electricity at a manufacturing cost of less than $1 per watt—a milestone in the solar energy industry. The company primarily provides solar technology to grid-tied solar power plants (or solar power plants that are connected to the utility grid) and commercial installations such as rooftop systems for factories. It plans to begin supplying modules to grid-connected homes beginning in 2009.

First Solar was founded in 1999. Its headquarters are in Tempe, Arizona, and its main factory is located in Ohio. Due to committed support of solar energy in Germany, First Solar built its second plant in Frankfurt, Germany. The company now has corporate offices in the United States and Europe and plans to open manufacturing plants in Malaysia. First Solar employs over four thousand people across the world.

Becoming an Engineer

Entry-level engineering positions require a bachelor's degree. States often require that engineers hold a license if their work affects public life or safety. When starting out, most beginning engineers work under the supervision of more experienced engineers. It is essential that engineers continue updating their education throughout their careers to keep up with new technological advances. Many go on to earn master's degrees or master of business administration (MBA) degrees in order to advance their career prospects.

Anyone who is interested in becoming an engineer should have an avid interest in science and math. Engineers must pay close attention to detail and solve problems using creativity and analytical thinking. Engineers are generally required to work as part of a team, often with specialists in a variety of different areas related to a project. An engineer must be highly proficient with computers and specialized technical software. Depending on an engineer's particular field, a day may be spent in a lab, at a manufacturing facility, or on-site at a solar installation.

Engineers employed in the field of solar energy work for equipment manufacturers, utility companies, research and development firms, consulting firms, and the government. Engineers who work in manufacturing may be involved in research and development or in day-to-day operations of production. Today, China, Germany, and Japan lead the world in solar cell manufacturing. It is expected, however, that the United States will increase production of solar technology as renewable energy use increases. Companies will hire engineers as well as metal workers, welders, mechanics, and other equipment operators and assemblers. In general, job prospects for many fields related to solar energy are highly favorable due to the growing market for renewable energy. Engineers entering the workplace currently have some of the highest starting salaries of any college graduates. For more information on the average salary for this job, and the other jobs mentioned in this book, please refer to the U.S. Bureau of Labor Statistics' *Occupational Outlook Handbook*, which can be found online.

Becoming a Solar Installer

As demand for solar energy increases, there will be more and more job openings for skilled technicians to install solar panels and other solar systems. For every huge solar power plant, such as Kramer Junction, there are many smaller installations that generate electricity for a single home, business, or other facility. PV cells are organized into modules, and modules are mounted in arrays—solar panels—made up of about four hundred PV cells. Ten to twenty arrays can provide enough electricity for one home. Newer homes may include building-integrated PV materials. In some places, a PV installation can be connected to the electric grid, and the owner can sell excess electricity from the installation to the utility company.

In addition to generating electricity, solar energy can be used to heat water, either for household use or to heat

A work crew installs solar electric panels on a residential rooftop in California. These solar panels will mean lower utility bills for the homeowner.

a swimming pool, and to heat a home through a solar radiant heating system. Technicians are needed to install and maintain these systems. PV and solar installers work with their clients from the planning phase to completion of construction work. Solar installers offer advice on an appropriate-sized system and help the client evaluate options. They must know the relevant building codes for the area and be able to obtain the necessary permits. They are also responsible for installing the panels or solar thermal system and connecting it to the electrical system. They may also do custom work or install a meter that records energy production.

Jobs in solar energy do not require a college degree, but people interested in careers in solar energy should acquire training, certification, and related expertise in the field. Electricians and contractors in the construction industry are well positioned to become solar installers, as well as people with experience in heating, air-conditioning, and refrigeration. Solar systems are becoming more technologically complex, and formal training in solar energy can help boost an aspiring solar installer's job prospects.

Training for jobs in the field of solar energy is available from a variety of institutions. Many universities, community colleges, and vocational/technical institutes offer programs in PV and solar thermal installation. Some renewable energy associations offer training programs for individuals interested in solar energy, and some corporations offer in-house training programs for their employees.

Solar installers can receive certification from the North American Board of Certified Energy Practitioners (NABCEP), a leading trade association in the field. NABCEP requires that certified installers meet certain requirements for experience or training, sign a code of ethics, and pass a written exam. The PV installer exam includes a variety of questions based on realistic scenarios that test the candidate's knowledge of topics such as system design, proper installation methods, safety, maintenance, and understanding of basic specs and plans.

A solar installer should also be self-motivated, good at solving problems, and willing to work hard to get the job done. Good people skills are necessary as well. You'll probably be working as part of a team, and you definitely want to have a good working relationship with the client.

Chapter Two

Wind Energy

Wind energy is a fast-growing field that holds great promise for anyone interested in a career in sustainable energy. Although wind energy currently accounts for just slightly over 1 percent of the nation's electricity, the Department of Energy aims to increase that figure to 6 percent by 2020. The American Wind Energy Association (AWEA) predicts that by 2030, wind could provide 20 percent of the nation's electricity. In 2007, wind energy development in the United States grew by 45 percent—a

Offshore wind turbine installations take advantage of winds that are faster and steadier than onshore winds.

faster pace than in any other nation in the world. The future of wind energy holds exciting prospects for utility companies, corporations, investors, property owners, and job seekers.

Wind energy is harnessed by wind turbines that consist of rotors (blades); an adjacent nacelle (enclosure) containing hardware such as a gearbox; a tower; and electronic equipment. The largest "utility-scale" wind turbines can each generate enough electricity for as many as 1,400 homes. These massive systems are mounted on 165 to 300 foot (50 to 90 meter) tall towers with rotors that are 165 to 300 feet (50 to 90 m) in diameter. Rotors for offshore turbines, which are situated in the ocean where the wind blows harder, can be as large as 360 feet (110 m) in diameter. Offshore turbines must be installed in relatively shallow water. Utility-scale turbines are usually installed on wind farms consisting of a large number of turbines.

Small wind turbines can be installed to provide electricity to homes and business and to power water pumps or communications equipment. In some cases, excess electricity generated by a wind turbine can be sold to the local utility company.

Wind energy is nonpolluting, sustainable, and efficient. It does not require fuel or produce waste. A wind energy system is cheaper to set up than a solar system. Wind farms can benefit rural economies, since landowners can lease out land for wind systems and still use the surrounding land for agriculture.

There are also disadvantages to wind energy. Not all areas receive enough wind to support wind energy development. According to the AWEA, the states with the highest wind energy potential are Iowa, Kansas, Minnesota, Montana, Nebraska, North Dakota, Oklahoma, South Dakota, Texas, and Wyoming. Texas is the top wind energy generating state in the United States, followed by Iowa and California.

Even in windy places, wind levels vary, and as a result, electricity production varies. On the flip side, excess electricity produced by wind generally cannot be stored. Wind turbines can be noisy, and some people consider wind farms ugly.

Wind energy is an emerging industry, and it is expected to create new jobs for workers with a wide range of backgrounds. Highly educated scientists, engineers, and researchers will make breakthroughs in turbine design, energy storage, and wind analysis. Workers will be needed in factories manufacturing rotors, towers, and other components. Technicians will be needed for the operation and maintenance of wind farms, as well as for the installation of new turbines. Nontechnical workers will handle the business and administrative side of wind energy, ranging from marketing to investing.

Scientists, Researchers, and Engineers

There are many research opportunities in wind energy, as scientists, engineers, and other researchers are looking to develop more efficient turbines and reduce costs. Changing the design of the blades, for example, can affect how the rotor catches the wind. Researchers are also working on technology that will be able to store

Members of the U.S. Department of Agriculture (USDA) Agricultural Research Service prepare to test experimental wind turbine blades.

wind energy. They are developing more efficient ways to integrate energy into the electric grid and transmit it to where it is needed. Researchers also look for ways to address issues and complaints concerning wind turbines. Today's turbines are quieter than older models. Researchers have also tested ways to prevent wind turbines from killing birds.

Jobs in wind energy research generally require at least a bachelor's degree in science, math, computer science, or engineering. Mechanical engineers, electrical engineers, and electronics engineers are in high demand for turbine manufacturing jobs as well as research positions. Engineers oversee the manufacturing of components such as blades, towers, gearboxes, and control systems. They also work on the installation, calibration, and testing of equipment in the field and analysis and evaluation of performance. Some universities offer programs specializing in wind energy. An MBA can also advance an engineer's career prospects.

Assessors: Scouting Out the Site

Before a wind system is installed, whether it's a utility-scale wind farm or a single turbine, a trained assessor performs a wind resource assessment of the area. The assessment includes information such as the best site for a wind system and an estimate of how much power the system will generate. An assessor takes into account factors such as wind speed, wind variability, wind direction, the surrounding landscape, and obstructions such as buildings or trees.

This wind turbine at the University of Minnesota–Morris provides half of the school's annual electricity. An agricultural economist holds a map identifying the best possible sites for wind turbines.

This job requires extensive fieldwork, as well as proficiency in computer modeling and mapping. A wind resource assessor may have a background in meteorology, science, engineering, or computer science.

Environmental Engineers

Potential wind turbine sites must also undergo an environmental impact assessment, which takes into account factors such as potential loss of habitat and effects on wildlife. Environmental concerns may be handled by an

Becoming a Wind Project Developer

Let's say you want to be a wind project developer. You have scouted out a windy area that you think would be the ideal place to set up wind turbines. What is the process for turning this idea into reality?

Set your goals. You could power your own house, sell electricity to your local utility company, or lease your land to a developer, such as a wind power plant.

Calculate your energy payback time. This is the amount of time it will take your installation to generate enough electricity to pay for manufacturing and construction costs.

Determine whether your site is appropriate for wind development. You can consult wind resource maps of your area and hire a professional to assess your land. He or she will also weigh factors such as zoning laws and proximity to power lines.

Figure out a business plan. You could develop the project yourself, work with partners, or lease the site to a developer.

Buy your turbine and other equipment. You'll need to decide what type of installation is appropriate for your site as well as what you can afford. Wind development may be eligible for government incentives.

Choose a reliable construction firm. Ask other people with wind installations for recommendations. Your construction manager will work out details such as building permits and compliance with regulations. Big wind farms typically take less than six months to build.

Don't forget to arrange a maintenance contract with a professional. Routine maintenance will maximize your turbines' electricity production.

environmental engineer. Environmental engineers specialize in areas such as waste management, pollution control, and land management. An environmental engineering program includes instruction in both physical and biological sciences. Workers with a background in biology or environmental science are also qualified to assess potential environmental impact.

Manufacturing and Technical Jobs

The growth of wind energy is increasingly creating new jobs for technicians and other workers with two-year degrees or other relevant training. Machinists and workers skilled in metalworking are required for manufacturing turbine blades, gearboxes, and towers. Electricians and other workers with electronics training are needed to produce the controls for wind turbines.

Wind farms are generally installed by construction crews and technicians working alongside engineers. Once the wind farm has been completed, wind farm technicians oversee its day-to-day operation and maintenance. They monitor the equipment, ensure compliance with regulations, and handle any dealings with contractors, authorities, and the public. Wind farm technicians should have experience working with electrical systems and be computer proficient.

Small wind systems are installed and maintained by technicians trained in wind energy and turbine technology. They must be knowledgeable in general electronics, mathematics, computers, and meteorology as well as the specific mechanics of wind turbines. Technicians in small

Engineers at the Alternative Energy Institute of West Texas A&M University perform service on a wind turbine 80 feet (24 m) above the ground. The turbine is located at a USDA Agricultural Research Service research station.

wind systems may also learn about business management and human relations.

Training for jobs in wind energy is not yet as widespread as training for jobs in solar energy. Nevertheless, the overall job outlook for this field is highly favorable. Technician programs are offered by some community colleges and other institutions. Graduates of these programs have excellent job prospects. Aspiring wind technicians can also look for apprenticeships and internships in the industry. The North American Board of Certified Energy Practitioners (NABCEP) is in the process of developing a certification program for small wind installers.

Chapter Three

Geothermal Energy, Hydropower, and Biofuels

Although solar and wind energy are the dominant renewable energy options, there are several other viable sources of renewable energy. These are geothermal, hydropower, and biomass energy. Many jobs in these fields are currently in research and development. These positions pay well, but they require extensive education and specialization.

The Calpine Sonoma power plant near Middletown, California, has harnessed geothermal energy since the 1960s. The plant's turbines are powered by steam that rushes up from inside the earth.

Geothermal Energy

Geothermal energy is energy derived from the earth's heat. The temperature of the earth's molten core is approximately 9,000 degrees Fahrenheit (5,000 degrees Celsius). This heat flows outward, creating underground reservoirs of hot water.

In some regions of the United States, these geothermal reservoirs can be tapped by wells to generate electricity. Alaska, Arizona, California, Colorado, Hawaii, Idaho, Montana, Nevada, New Mexico, Oregon, Utah, Washington, and Wyoming have reservoirs with the potential for geothermal development. In fact, California gets 5 percent of its energy from geothermal reservoirs. Overall, only about 4 percent of renewable energy in the United States comes from geothermal sources—a miniscule proportion of total energy consumption. Power plants under development will increase the amount of electricity generated from geothermal energy.

In addition to large-scale electricity production, geothermal energy can provide heating and cooling for homes and other buildings. In areas with geothermal reservoirs, wells can bring hot water up to ground level. This type of direct heating system can be used for industrial processes as well as heating. Even in areas without geothermal reservoirs, geothermal energy can be accessed using a heat pump. Throughout the United States, the ground maintains an average temperature of 50–60°F (10–15°C) year-round—warmer than the air temperature in the winter and cooler than the temperature of the air in the summer. The heat pump, which is buried in the ground, takes advantage of this temperature difference. In the winter, it transfers heat from the earth to someone's home or other building. In the summer, this is reversed: the heat pump takes heat from the home and transfers it underground. The pump can use this excess heat to provide hot water. Geothermal energy is clean and limitless, and unlike wind and solar energy, it does not vary with the weather or time of day.

Being an Electrician

Electricians are crucial figures in every area of alternative energy, including geothermal energy. Electricians install and maintain the wiring and other electrical components in power plants, businesses, factories, and residences. At every solar power plant, wind farm, and geothermal power plant, electricians perform the hands-on work that allows electricity to start flowing. Any homeowner interested in installing solar panels or a small wind turbine will require the services of an electrician.

Most electricians receive their training through apprenticeship programs that combine classroom instruction with supervised on-the-job work. They learn to read blueprints, comply with electric codes, draw diagrams, and install electrical components using a variety of tools. Most states require that electricians be licensed, and experienced and highly trained electricians can receive certification as master electricians.

The job market is favorable for electricians. They generally work a forty hour week. Work environment varies widely—electricians may work on a construction site, in a factory, or at a power plant.

Geothermal Energy Jobs

Geothermal energy development has great potential for job creation. Scientists and engineers will be needed to research new geothermal reservoirs. Workers will be needed for the construction and operation of new geothermal power plants. Skilled technicians will be needed for installation and maintenance of heat pumps.

Many people believe, incorrectly, that geothermal energy is still in the experimental stages of development. In fact, there are functioning geothermal power plants in more than ten states. Still, as with every form of renewable energy, research is being conducted with the goal of improving and expanding geothermal energy production. Scientists and engineers continue to explore emerging applications of geothermal energy. For example, research is being conducted in the area of enhanced geothermal systems (EGS). These would generate electricity from hot, dry rock deep in the earth, rather than through geothermal reservoirs of water.

Scientists and Engineers

Highly trained scientists and engineers are needed to identify new geothermal reservoirs, construct geothermal facilities, and oversee operations at geothermal power plants. Most jobs in these areas require graduate degrees and previous work experience.

Geologists are scientists who study and analyze the rocks and rock formations in an area. They spend a great deal of time outdoors collecting samples and measurements, and they also perform lab tests to determine the content of the samples. After analyzing the data, a geologist will make recommendations on whether a potential site is worth developing for geothermal energy.

Geophysicists—scientists who study the properties of the earth—explore and map the reservoir area using specialized equipment. Geophysicists do some work outdoors, but they also spend a great deal of time at the computer doing modeling and analysis. Most geophysicists specialize in a particular type of geological system.

Geochemists are scientists who study the chemical composition of water, soil, and rock samples. Hydrologists study the occurrence, distribution, circulation, and properties of underground and surface water. When it comes to geothermal energy, hydrologists take measurements and collect specific data, such as the flow of the steam and hot water in the reservoir. Geologists, geophysicists, geochemists, and hydrologists will all make recommendations regarding drilling into the reservoir, constructing the plant, and managing energy production.

Building Geothermal Power Plants

Before a plant is built, environmental engineers and biologists perform an environmental impact assessment. There are four different types of commercial geothermal power plants, all of which generate electricity from the heat in geothermal reservoirs. Constructing a geothermal power plant employs engineers from a variety of disciplines, including electrical and mechanical engineers, as well as hydraulic, structural, and geothermal reservoir engineers.

Geothermal energy can be tapped for heating and cooling buildings. Here, workers install a geothermal system at a hospital in Elgin, Illinois.

Hydraulic engineers specialize in projects that involve controlling water. They direct and design water transporting facilities and equipment, such as water mains, tanks, turbines, and pumps. Structural engineers design the structure of the power plant, from the foundation and supports to the framework of the buildings. They ensure that the plant is safe and compliant with codes and regulations. Geothermal reservoir engineers work to maximize the production of energy from a geothermal reservoir. If a geothermal reservoir is managed improperly, it shortens the amount of time that the reservoir will remain productive. Geothermal reservoir engineers help design the power plant, monitor its operations, and analyze data in order to predict the future performance of the reservoir. They also fix problems and design new projects to further develop the reservoir.

In addition, surveyors, electricians, construction and drilling equipment operators, and other skilled workers such as plumbers and welders are needed for the construction of a new facility. Once a power plant is running, engineers and technicians oversee day-to-day operations and ensure compliance with government regulations.

HVAC Engineers

Heating, ventilating, and air-conditioning (HVAC) engineers and contractors work in both geothermal electricity generation and in heat pump installation and maintenance. Every year, fifty to sixty thousand new heat pumps are installed in homes and other buildings. The system is installed by a construction team that includes engineers, excavators, and other contractors.

Workers carry out their jobs at the Rapidan dam in Rapidan, Minnesota. The dam was built approximately 100 years ago, and it is still generating hydroelectricity today.

HVAC professionals test, maintain, repair, and upgrade heat pump systems as needed. They must be familiar with the equipment and proficient at using various hand and power tools. HVAC training and certification is available at many community colleges. In addition, the Association of Energy Engineers (AEE) offers a Certified GeoExchange Designer program. This program enables heat pump engineers and technicians with a bachelor's degree, a technical degree, or relevant experience to earn certification at various levels.

The Environmental Impact of Hydroelectric Power

Hydroelectric power often comes with a high environmental cost. Damming a river can devastate populations of fish and other organisms. Fish that migrate upstream and downstream, such as salmon, can be particularly affected. Plants and animals that live near the river lose their habitats. Reservoir water tends to stagnate, sometimes causing the spread of algae and weeds. Larger dams cause greater environmental disruption—for instance, the construction of the Hoover Dam between Arizona and Nevada created Lake Mead, which is 110 miles (177 kilometers) long.

Because of the environmental consequences of hydroelectric development, hydroelectric energy is not expected to match the levels of job growth of other renewable energy sources. Still, hydroelectric energy generates a significant percentage of the nation's electricity, and requires a sizeable workforce to maintain and operate facilities.

Jobs in Hydropower

Hydroelectric power is the cheapest and most prevalent form of renewable energy in the United States. It accounts for about 10 percent of the nation's electricity, nearly ten times the amount generated by all other forms of renewable energy combined.

Hydroelectric power is produced by using moving water to generate electricity. In the most common type of hydroelectric power project, a dam is constructed across a river. Water behind the dam is stored in a reservoir. When water is released from the reservoir, it turns a turbine that generates electricity. There are about 2,400 dams in the United States that produce electricity. Hydroelectric power does not require fuel and it does not pollute. As long as the water supply remains constant—drought can affect river levels—it is a limitless source of energy.

Conventional hydroelectric power plants employ scientists, engineers, plant operators, electricians, and technicians. Hydrologists, hydraulic engineers, and hydraulic technicians are especially important for hydroelectric plant operations. Hydrologists study the water supply and deal with issues such as flood control, water quality, and compliance with environmental regulations. They spend a great deal of time in the field mapping waterways, identifying water supplies, and designing projects. Hydrologists also perform lab work and create computer models. Hydraulic engineers and technicians design and maintain the plants.

When a new plant is constructed, it provides job opportunities for biologists and environmental engineers, who assess the site for impact on wildlife and the river course. Civil, structural, and hydraulic engineers design and oversee

38

the construction of dams and facilities. Mechanical and electrical engineers plan and design systems that produce power. Construction crews are needed to build the new plant. Today, scientists and researchers are working on development of innovative turbine designs that take environmental effects into account. These turbines might not require a dam, and they would not harm fish and other wildlife.

Future Careers in Hydropower

There are exciting research opportunities in hydroelectric energy, both in improving conventional hydroelectric technology and in developing new methods of generating hydroelectricity. Research into a form of energy known as hydrokinetic energy could someday lead to the construction of power facilities that tap into the energy in moving water. These facilities could generate power from waves, ocean tides, and river currents. Unlike wind or solar energy, there is little variability in the pounding of ocean waves. There are many different research areas in harnessing hydrokinetic energy. Wave energy, for example, can be captured by buoys that generate electricity directly or turn a turbine. Tidal energy can turn turbines when the tide rises and falls.

Today, experimental hydrokinetic energy projects employ scientists, engineers, and other researchers. Hydrokinetic energy is not yet developed enough to generate a significant amount of electricity in the United States. If researchers succeed in developing a cheap and efficient system for harnessing hydrokinetic energy, it could prove a significant source of renewable energy. Building and maintaining a hydrokinetic system would require a workforce ranging from engineers to construction workers.

Biomass energy is an expanding field that employs many scientists. Here, a researcher at the National Renewable Energy Laboratory (NREL) analyzes algae samples.

Jobs in Biomass Energy

Since prehistoric times, humans have used biomass energy by burning wood for cooking and heat. Biomass includes trees, grasses, food crops, waste products from agriculture and forestry, and organic waste products from industry and municipalities. Methane emitted by rotting garbage in landfills even qualifies as a fuel produced by biomass.

Biomass energy is renewable and plentiful. It can easily be converted into fuel for vehicles, which gives it an advantage over some other promising sources of alternative energy. Unlike fossil fuels, biofuels used for transportation or power generation do not increase carbon dioxide levels in the atmosphere. This is because burning fossil fuels releases carbon dioxide that has been stored underground for millions of years. The carbon dioxide released from biofuels is already part of the earth's carbon cycle.

Biomass energy is still in the early stages of development, and researchers must overcome a number of obstacles before it becomes a cheap and efficient energy source. Ethanol and biodiesel, the leading biofuels, are primarily made from corn and soybeans. (Brazil, a leading biofuel producer, uses sugarcane as a fuel source.) Many experts have grown concerned that growth of biofuel production could contribute to food shortages. Also, fossil fuel energy is expended planting, cultivating, harvesting, and processing the biofuel. Some people question whether biofuel is worth the resources spent in its production.

Rising gas prices through 2008 led to a boom in ethanol and biodiesel production and research. Gasoline contains about 10 percent ethanol, and the alternative fuel

This biomass boiler burns corn kernels. It provides heat for a number of greenhouses used in a small business.

E-85 contains 85 percent ethanol. Biodiesel can be substituted for regular diesel fuel in vehicles and generators that burn diesel. Researchers are working to produce biofuels cheaply and efficiently from sources other than food crops. Fast-growing grasses and agricultural waste, such as corn stalks, can be processed into cellulosic ethanol, though the method is not yet ready for large-scale production. As an alternative to soybeans, algae can yield high amounts of oil for biodiesel.

Biomass can also be used to generate electricity. Biomass can be burnt to produce steam, which turns a turbine, or it can be added to coal or other fossil fuels in conventional power plants. Wells drilled in landfills can pump out methane used in electricity production.

Workers are also needed to construct and operate biomass energy plants. This includes both power plants and biorefineries—just as oil is processed in a refinery, biomass is processed in a biorefinery. Scientists, researchers, engineers, technicians, plumbers, operators, and construction workers are all required to bring a biomass energy plant to operation.

Farmers and Agricultural Engineers

Biomass energy production can provide jobs and economic opportunities in rural areas. Farmers who grow corn and soybeans—and who may someday switch to fast-growing "bioenergy feedstocks"—provide the raw materials for biofuels. They may be small farmers who have farmed the same land for generations or the managers of huge corporate farms. Farmers generally study agriculture at a two-year college or at a university, taking courses such as agricultural production and horticulture as well as business and economics.

Agricultural engineers are engineers who apply scientific principals to the production and handling of crops. Agriculture is a challenging field because of fluctuations in the market as well as in crop yield. A biofuels market, especially a market that encourages sustainable farming practices, could increase demand for crops and create jobs without harming the environment. These jobs include building, operating, and maintaining new facilities, which would support farmers and stimulate the local economy.

Chapter Four

Sustainable Energy and Transportation

Every day, the United States uses up about twenty-one million barrels of oil, much of it imported from other countries. Over two-thirds of this oil is used in the transportation sector, producing pollution that includes greenhouse gases. About a third of all greenhouse gases are emitted by automobiles and other vehicles. Creating energy efficient vehicles makes environmental and economic sense. Developing green technologies and vehicles will create jobs in the short term, and it will make the American automobile industry more competitive in the long term.

Automobiles and other vehicles can be powered by a number of renewable fuels. This automobile runs on electricity instead of gasoline.

New Automobile Technologies, New Careers

Shifting to hybrid vehicles, electric vehicles, and vehicles powered by hydrogen fuel cells would benefit the environment and reduce demand for foreign oil. These technologies use less gasoline or rely altogether on new sources of fuel. In the long run, such vehicles would also make economic sense. Oil reserves will eventually run out. Right now, the United States has the opportunity to develop new automobile technologies before that happens.

Such a shift would transform the automobile industry and create a variety of new jobs. Most jobs are currently in research and development. Eventually, a wave of jobs will be created in manufacturing. Automotive engineers— mechanical engineers who design, develop, and manufacture vehicles and their components—will benefit from a solid working knowledge of green technologies. Mechanics can receive training on how to service and repair hybrid vehicles, which require expertise in electronics and car computers. There will be opportunities in sales and marketing for business-oriented individuals who are interested in promoting alternative green vehicles and interacting with potential customers. Just about anyone following a career path in the automotive industry will have a competitive edge in the job market if they're familiar with alternative fuel vehicles.

Advanced Batteries

Many experts agree that developing compact, efficient, affordable batteries is critical to filling future energy needs. The need for improved energy storage systems ranges from utility-scale power plants down to electronics that we use in our daily lives. There is currently no practical means of storage for wind and solar-generated electricity. An effective storage system could store energy when solar or wind sources generated excess electricity, then provide it to consumers during periods of peak electricity demand. On a day-to-day level, people demand that electronic devices such as computers, cell phones, and cordless tools allow longer periods of use before needing to be recharged. In the future, cutting-edge batteries will be essential to producing hybrid and electric vehicles.

There is no "one size fits all" solution to the issue of energy storage. A number of different chemicals can be used in constructing batteries, which generate electricity as a result of chemical reactions. Lithium ion batteries are used in laptop computers. Lead-acid batteries are currently used in most automobiles. The Toyota Prius, a hybrid car powered by an electric battery as well as an engine that burns gasoline, uses a nickel-metal-hydride battery. Utility companies are testing huge sodium-sulfur batteries to store energy generated from solar and wind power plants. There are advantages and drawbacks to every type in terms of cost, safety, ability to hold a charge, and other factors.

Some of the most ambitious and intensive areas of research and development are in advanced batteries for automobiles. Today's hybrid vehicles use both an electric battery and an internal combustion engine. Some experts predict that, as battery technology improves, vehicles will become less reliant on the internal combustion engine. In the future, the internal combustion engine—and the need for gasoline—may be eliminated. Vehicles could rely

Hybrid vehicles achieve much higher gas mileage than vehicles that are solely powered by gasoline. Here, a plug-in model Toyota Prius Hybrid recharges.

completely on batteries that can be recharged by plugging them into an electric outlet, just like cell phones.

The most promising battery type for automobiles is the lithium-ion battery, but it is still not ready for the road. Cars are larger and demand more power than laptops and cell phones, though scale is only part of the problem. A car battery is put under more stress than a battery used in a small electronic device—it must withstand conditions such as extreme heat and cold, rough treatment, dust, and moisture. The optimal battery will have to make trade-offs in terms of safety, reliability,

Transportation Goes Green

Many people are turning toward alternate means of transportation rather than relying solely on their cars. This creates new business niches and the possibility of growth in some job areas.

People who live in urban areas may sign up for a car sharing service. They can reserve a car for a specific time slot and pick it up at a location in their neighborhood. Car sharing is a growing trend, and companies such as Zipcar are prospering.

Some commuters are turning to public transportation, such as buses and trains. Urban transit systems are expanding, and expansion requires workers such as urban planners, construction workers, and operators.

More and more people are choosing to ride a bicycle when going to work or running errands. Many cities are becoming more bike friendly, providing bike lanes and bike storage facilities. This trend is good news for bicycle shops and repair services.

cost, and capacity. Nanotechnology, which deals with materials on a molecular level, has the potential to lead to breakthroughs in next generation batteries. Nano-engineered materials show promise in improving battery performance.

Government policy makers, auto manufacturers, and battery companies all strongly support the development of advanced batteries. During the mid-1990s, the American automobile industry sidelined research and development of electric and hybrid vehicles, and the Japanese auto-makers Honda and Toyota came to dominate the market. Today, the leading battery producers are South Korea and Japan. The United States is anxious to catch up and prove itself a world leader in battery development and manufacturing.

The government, private investors, and large corpora-tions alike are strongly supporting advanced battery research and production. The government and companies such as GM operate laboratories focusing on batteries. Batteries also offer opportunities for innovative start-up companies. In 2009, the battery company A123Systems announced a plan to build a lithium-ion battery factory in Michigan, which would employ one hundred people. A123Systems expects to eventually employ fourteen thou-sand people at U.S. facilities. It is probable that other companies will also expand as battery technology improves and reaches the market.

Currently, most of the jobs in advanced batteries are related to research, development, and testing. This stage requires highly educated scientists, engineers, and other researchers.

General Motors unveiled a new lithium-ion battery in 2009. The company is planning to manufacture these batteries for an electric car, known as the Volt, which it is developing.

A day at work might include testing to see how much heat is generated by the battery or simulating tests to determine how the battery might behave in a vehicle. Advanced battery engineers and scientists also develop and test new materials, evaluate and work on improving battery life, research ways to reduce costs, and facilitate commercialization of successful products. Many labs offer opportunities for postdoctoral researchers and students.

The job market in batteries will expand when companies begin manufacturing more products. This will require new facilities or expansion of existing facilities, which will provide jobs for architects, engineers, construction crews, and other workers in building trades. Manufacturing jobs will require skilled technicians as well as unskilled workers who will be trained on the job. Workers will be needed for jobs associated with battery production, as well as manufacturing electrical systems for vehicles, battery components, and computer software.

Hydrogen Fuel Cells

There is another potential energy source for automobiles that is virtually nonpolluting, limitless in availability, and more efficient than an internal combustion engine. This fuel is hydrogen, the most plentiful chemical element in the universe. Although vehicles powered by fuel cells have been tested successfully, there are many hurdles in the way of mass production.

Like a battery, a hydrogen fuel cell produces electricity through a chemical reaction. Hydrogen gas (H_2) combines with oxygen (O_2) to form water (H_2O), generating heat and electricity in the process. Instead of a gasoline tank, hydrogen fuel cell vehicles have a hydrogen gas tank that stores the fuel. Vehicles powered by hydrogen fuel cells do not pollute—the only byproduct is water, usually emitted as vapor. Unlike batteries, hydrogen fuel cells do not have to be recharged.

Researchers will have to overcome many obstacles before hydrogen fuel cell vehicles can become a viable product. The most basic dilemma is cost. The price of fuel cells cannot yet compete with conventional vehicles. Another issue is storing and transporting hydrogen gas, a flammable fuel. Large volumes of hydrogen are required to power a vehicle, so the gas is generally stored in a pressurized tank. Refueling vehicles and supplying filling stations with fuel would be a very different process with hydrogen than with gasoline.

Another major issue concerns the production of hydrogen. Hydrogen occurs naturally as a component of chemicals such as water, fossil fuel, or biomass. In order to produce hydrogen gas, it must be extracted from one of these sources. Hydrogen is not truly a clean energy source unless it is produced using renewable energy sources. Currently, most hydrogen is produced from natural gas—which is a fossil fuel—using a process that requires energy input and releases carbon dioxide. Researchers are exploring ways to extract hydrogen using renewable energy. Possibilities include splitting water molecules to release hydrogen using wind energy or solar energy. The biological activity of some microorganisms can also produce hydrogen as a byproduct.

Switching to a "hydrogen economy" in transportation would require a massive nationwide infrastructure project. This may include construction of a network of pipelines

The first public hydrogen filling station opened in Los Angeles, California, in 2008. Filling stations such as this one may become commonplace if hydrogen-powered automobiles catch on.

carrying hydrogen across the country, but it is possible that technology could be developed that would allow the production of hydrogen on-site at filling stations. Hydrogen storage facilities would also have to be built. If hydrogen became a cheap, efficient, and clean energy source, its uses would also be expanded to include stationary fuel cells that would supply power to homes and other buildings. Fuel cells could even be developed that would power cell phones and other small electronic devices.

It will probably be years before fuel cell vehicles enter the market. Even if the technology succeeds, it will take much longer for the establishment of a hydrogen infrastructure. In the meantime, most jobs are in research being conducted at universities, government laboratories, and manufacturing research and development departments. Engineers are in high demand, since fuel cell research involves electrochemical, chemical, electrical, mechanical, and materials science engineering. For students interested in hydrogen fuel cells, many universities have innovative institutes and departments devoted to hydrogen fuel cells and related research. If fuel cells prove to be the key to the future of transportation, the new industry will require a huge workforce in fuel cell manufacturing and related fields.

Chapter Five

Related Careers in Sustainable Energy

As the green energy industry expands, it is expected to create a number of career opportunities both directly and indirectly related to sustainable energy. There are careers, for example, in energy efficiency—the reduction of energy used for a certain task and the resultant reduction in the impact of conventional fossil fuels. White-collar workers, such as managers and sales representatives, are required to handle the business side of

Advances in solar cells may make solar energy more popular in the United States and around the world.

alternative energy companies. The potential future development of a "smart" electrical grid, which would save money by increasing energy efficiency, would also create a variety of new jobs.

Energy Management

Energy management analysts, engineers, and technicians work to improve the efficiency of systems that use energy. Energy efficiency is the use of technology to reduce energy use without sacrificing energy services. Most vehicles, heating systems, and appliances—essentially any device that uses energy—can be improved in some way so that they consume less energy. A new refrigerator model, for example, will use less energy than an older model if it has more insulation and a tighter sealing door. A house will have lower heating and air-conditioning bills if there are no leaks, such as inadequately insulated walls or gaps in the foundation, where air can escape. Energy efficient systems cost less and help protect the environment. In addition, research into energy efficiency encourages innovation that often leads to additional improvements of the product.

Energy research technicians work in research and development in laboratories and manufacturing facilities. They work closely with engineers and scientists to develop energy efficient systems. The Environmental Protection Agency designates energy efficient appliances with an Energy Star label.

Energy production technicians install, maintain, and repair large systems such as temperature control systems.

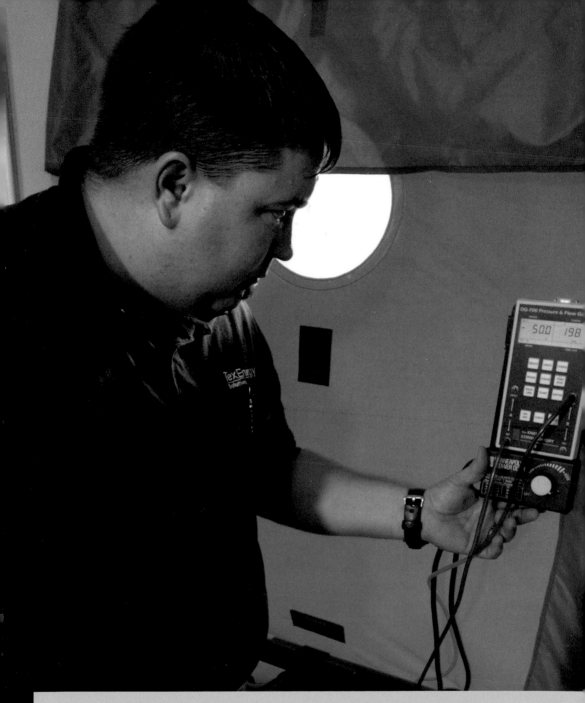

This project manager for TexEnergy Solutions in Fort Worth, Texas, tests a home for drafts. Making a house more energy efficient can reduce heating and cooling costs.

Much of their work is done in large facilities, such as power plants and factories. The job requires both mechanical aptitude and training in electronics.

Energy analysts, sometimes called energy conservation technicians, perform energy audits of homes and other

Profile: Steven Chu, Secretary of Energy

In 2009, President Barack Obama appointed Dr. Steven Chu Secretary of Energy. Dr. Chu considers climate change an issue of critical importance and he has worked to raise awareness of the potentially catastrophic consequences of climate change. Dr. Chu has conducted research into alternative energy, including solar energy and biofuels, and he aims to end dependence on foreign oil. President Obama's ambitious energy agenda would incorporate all of these priorities and create millions of jobs.

Before being named secretary of energy, Dr. Chu was director of the Lawrence Berkeley National Laboratory at the University of California, Berkeley, and professor of physics and molecular and cell biology. At the Berkeley Laboratory, Dr. Chu brought people together from a variety of disciplines—such as physics, material science, and chemistry—to work collaboratively on projects related to sustainable energy.

Dr. Chu earned a mathematics degree and a physics degree from the University of Rochester, and a Ph.D. in physics from the University of California, Berkeley. He worked at Bell Labs and taught physics at Stanford University before taking the position at UC Berkeley. Dr. Chu has received numerous awards and distinctions, including a Guggenheim Fellowship and the 1997 Nobel Prize in Physics.

structures. They analyze energy use and energy cost, and they suggest ways to improve a building's overall energy efficiency. For instance, an energy analyst might recommend replacing a building's old, drafty windows with new tinted windows that reduce air-conditioning costs by reflecting sunlight. Energy analysts examine furnaces, ductwork, appliances, and the building's exterior. They may correct the problem themselves or make recommendations. Utility companies often send out energy analysts to assess customer's homes. Some energy analysts are also trained in renewable energy and can make recommendations on installing solar panels or other renewable energy systems.

Large corporations are now recognizing the benefits of energy efficiency. Wal-Mart has opened a pilot store in Las Vegas, Nevada, that uses 45 percent less energy than most stores of the same size. New federal regulations, financial incentives, and public concern could spur other corporations and industries to adopt energy efficient policies as well.

Creating a Smart Electric Grid

The nation's electric grid is the infrastructure that transmits electricity across long distances and distributes it to customers. The electric grid as it exists today grew haphazardly over the course of the twentieth century. As a result, it consists of a patchwork of local and regional systems that is difficult to navigate. The entire country isn't even unified into a single grid—there are four grids in the United States that are not interconnected.

A technician monitors an electric power distribution grid in Pennsylvania. A smart grid could eliminate many problems that current power grids have, such as large-scale blackouts.

Distance presents another problem for connecting renewable energy sources to the grids. Major power plants convey electricity across high voltage transmission lines. Renewable energy sources, such as wind farms, are often located in remote areas far away from existing high voltage transmission lines. Constructing these lines can require a major investment.

A "smart grid" would address this issue and many other drawbacks to the current grid. The creation of a smart grid is sometimes compared to the construction of the interstate highway system or to the development of the Internet. New transmission lines would bring alternate energy sources such as solar, wind, and geothermal power into the grid. However, this physical infrastructure is just one aspect of the smart grid.

New information technology in the smart grid would allow the grid to diagnose and respond to a disruption, making it "self-healing." This aspect of the smart grid would address national security concerns. Today, a terrorist attack or natural disaster that impacts part of the grid could have repercussions across an entire region. A smart grid could ensure that damage or disturbances to the grid will be contained. There are many ways that a smart grid would be more reliable. According to the Department of Energy, power outages cost the nation $150 billion annually. Utility companies often have to rely on customers to learn about power outages. The smart grid would be able to monitor and control electricity flow. This could prevent power outages and save the nation a lot of money. The smart grid would also be more efficient, capable of meeting demand for electricity without the construction of new power plants that are used only during peak consumer demand.

The smart grid would also engage consumers and encourage energy efficient habits. One potential innovation would be the installation of smart meters in homes and businesses that monitor hour-to-hour electricity use. The pricing structure for electricity would change to variable "real time" prices announced hours or days ahead. Consumers could save money by using less electricity during higher priced periods. Conceivably, smart appliances linked to the smart meter could automatically switch to a low energy level during higher priced hours. Solar panels and small wind turbines could easily be connected to the meter. Someday, this system could also support the widespread use of electric cars. People could recharge their cars cheaply during the night, when electricity demand—and therefore, prices—would be lower.

The development, construction, and management of a smart grid would create many jobs for skilled workers across the country. Engineers, designers, and construction workers would be needed to build new transmission lines and related facilities. Manufacturers would be needed to provide equipment for construction projects. Computer and information technology specialists would design and implement new digital information systems. This job would carry enormous responsibility, since information technology experts would also put cybersecurity measures in place to prevent hackers from accessing the grid. Grid operators would oversee day-to-day operations. More jobs would be created, too, as innovators develop new improvements to the smart grid.

The effects of coal mining can devastate the environment. In mountaintop removal mining, up to 1,000 feet (305 m) of a mountain is blasted away with explosives in order to reach coal seams underneath.

Another Look at Fossil Fuels

Renewable energy sources offer solutions that could some-day guarantee an environmentally stable and energy independent future. In the meantime, however, the United States remains heavily reliant on fossil fuels to meet its energy needs. As the nation makes the transition toward renewable energy, it also makes economic and environmental sense to reduce pollution and other impacts of fossil fuel use.

One of the most controversial approaches is the development of "clean coal" technology. Coal is the cheapest and most abundant fossil fuel, generating about half of the electricity in the United States, but it is also the dirtiest. Burning coal emits over a hundred pollutants into the air and water, including sulfur dioxide, carbon dioxide, and mercury.

Clean coal technologies would reduce pollution emitted by coal-fired power plants, though most are not yet commercially available. The most widely discussed clean coal technology is carbon capture and storage (CCS). Instead of being released into the atmosphere, carbon dioxide is captured and injected into underground reservoirs. At the time of this writing, there have been no large-scale tests of CCS.

Another clean coal technology is the development of integrated gasification combined cycle (IGCC) technology. Coal fired IGCC plants convert coal into a gas before using it to produce electricity. IGCC power plants are more expensive than regular coal plants but they emit less pollution. Theoretically, IGCC plants would be better able to capture carbon dioxide. There are two IGCC power plants in the United States. Other potential clean coal technologies include improved turbine technology in coal power plants and fuel cells powered by coal gas.

Many environmentalists believe that there is no such thing as clean coal. Clean coal technologies address pollutants emitted by coal power, but they do not address the environmental impact of coal mining. Coal mining devastates forests and waterways, destroying vital plant and animal habitats. Environmentalists also claim that money being spent on clean coal research would be better directed toward renewable energy development. In addition, they point out the many obstacles confronting clean coal technologies, including high costs, the dangers of storing carbon dioxide underground, and the difficulty of safely disposing of waste generated by coal power.

Clean coal technology now employs scientists, engineers, and other researchers. If the technology does prove viable, implementing new projects would require a workforce to equip conventional power plants with CCS technology and to construct and operate new power plants.

Supporting Sustainable Energy

Renewable energy employs people with a variety of skills and work backgrounds. For every technical job installing wind turbines, and every scientific job designing new solar modules, there are executives and administrators who run the business aspect of renewable energy. White-collar workers do not need to know the technical details of the field, but their job does require a broad understanding of the technology.

Chief executives and high level officers in large renewable energy corporations generally hold an MBA or economics degree and have extensive business experience. The executives of large companies earn very large salaries, but they must work very hard to get to the top.

Large corporations will hire personnel in marketing, sales, advertising, customer relations, human resources, and accounting. They will need technical writers, computer network administrators, and department managers. Most of these jobs require four-year degrees. Employers look for people who are enthusiastic about renewable energy and eager to learn about the field and keep up-to-date on new developments in the industry.

Nonprofit Careers

In addition to jobs related to business and research, there are job possibilities in nonprofit groups, professional associations, and other independent organizations involved in energy and environmental causes. The National Resources Defense Council, for example, focuses on causes such as curbing global warming and building a clean energy economy. There are many other organizations on national, state, and local levels that work to address environmental concerns, including advocacy of renewable energy. Volunteering at a nonprofit organization related to sustainable energy is a great way to gain experience and learn about the field. Likewise, many nonprofit organizations offer internship opportunities.

An energy educator for a nonprofit organization demonstrates a mini wind turbine and solar panel in Detroit, Michigan.

Teaching

Good communicators who are passionate about sharing their renewable energy vision with others may decide to choose teaching as a career. Teaching opportunities range from specialized professorships in universities to technical training programs in two-year schools to junior high math and science curriculum. A teaching job generally requires a four-year degree and licensing. Teaching is challenging work that requires patience, dedication, and expertise, but most teachers say that the rewards are well worth the effort.

Glossary

apprenticeship When a person gets training for a career by working for someone who is accomplished in that trade. Apprenticeships can include classroom training.

bioenergy Electricity or fuel derived from biomass.

biomass Organic material, especially plant life, that can be converted into energy.

blueprint A print or reproduction of a drawing or other image containing symbols and notations necessary to create an electrical system. Blueprints are also known as electrical prints.

calibration The process of making fine adjustments to an instrument.

current A flow of electric charge, such as through an electrical wire.

electric grid The transmission lines, power stations, and other infrastructure that distribute electricity.

energy efficiency A reduction of energy used for a service—such as lighting—that does not diminish the quality of the service.

fuel cell A device that produces electricity as a result of a chemical reaction involving a fuel, such as hydrogen.

geothermal Pertaining to the interior heat of the earth.

hydroelectric Relating to the production of electricity from flowing water.

hydrokinetic Pertaining to the motion of fluids.

incentive A motivation, such as the promise of a payment, which encourages a person, business, or organization to do something.

innovation The introduction of something new, such as a product, idea, or method.

master of business administration (MBA) A graduate degree in business.

module A standardized component that is assembled into a unit with other such components.

photovoltaic Relating to energy produced by exposure to light.

renewable energy Energy from sources that are naturally replenished.

semiconductor A material that conducts electricity but not as well as metals. Semiconductor materials are used as a base for computer chips and photovoltaic cells.

silicon A nonmetallic chemical element that is useful in industry because of its properties as a semiconductor.

turbine A machine containing a rotor that is turned by moving fluid, steam, or air. The kinetic energy of the fluid, steam, or air is thus transformed into mechanical energy, which is used to generate electricity.

For More Information

American Solar Energy Society
2400 Central Avenue
Suite A
Boulder, CO 80301
(303) 443-3130
Web site: http://www.ases.org
The American Solar Energy Society is the nation's
    leading association of solar professionals and grass-
    roots advocates.

American Wind Energy Association
1101 14th Street NW, 12th Floor
Washington, DC 20005
(202) 383-2500
Web site: http://www.awea.org
This trade and advocacy group is dedicated to promot-
    ing wind power growth.

Apollo Alliance
330 Townsend Street, Suite 205
San Francisco, CA 94107
(415) 371-1700
Web site: http://apolloalliance.org
This coalition of labor, business, environmental, and
    community leaders works to catalyze a clean energy
    revolution that will put millions of Americans to work
    in a new generation of high-quality, green-collar jobs.

Canadian Renewable Energy Industry
Industry Canada
C.D. Howe Building
235 Queen Street
Ottawa, ON K1A 0H5
Canada
Web site: http://www.ic.gc.ca
This branch of Industry Canada supports the develop-
    ment and demonstration of renewable energy
    technologies.

Canadian Wind Energy Association
Suite 810, 170 Laurier Avenue
West Ottawa, ON K1P 5V5
Canada
(800) 922-6932
Web site: http://www.canwea.ca
This organization is dedicated to promoting the develop-
    ment of wind energy in Canada.

North American Board of Certified Energy Practitioners
10 Hermes Road, Suite 400
Malta, NY 12020
(518) 899-8186
Web site: http://www.nabcep.org
This organization offers certifications and certificate
    programs to renewable energy professionals through-
    out North America.

Rocky Mountain Institute
2317 Snowmass Creek Road

Snowmass, CO 81654
(970) 927-3851
Web site: http://www.rmi.org
This nonprofit organization works to foster the efficient
    and restorative use of energy and other resources.

Web Sites

Due to the changing nature of Internet links, Rosen
Publishing has developed an online list of Web sites
related to the subject of this book. This site is updated
regularly. Please use this link to access the list:

http://www.rosenlinks.com/gca/ener

For Further Reading

Bowman, Ron. *The Green Guide to Power: Thinking Outside the Grid*. North Charleston, SC: BookSurge Publishing, 2008.

Cassio, Jim, and Alice Rush. *Green Careers: Choosing Work for a Sustainable Future*. Gabriola Island, BC, Canada: New Society Publishers, 2009.

Chung, Laura Walker. *Vault Career Guide to the Energy Industry*. New York, NY: Vault, 2005.

Croston, Glenn. *75 Green Businesses You Can Start to Make Money and Make a Difference*. Irvine, CA: Entrepreneur Press, 2008.

DeAngelis, Therese, ed. *Green Jobs for a New Economy: The College and Career Guide to Emerging Opportunities*. Princeton, NJ: Peterson's, 2010.

DeGalan, Julie, and Bryon Middlekauff. *Great Jobs for Environmental Studies Majors*. New York, NY: McGraw Hill, 2008.

Dukert, Joseph M. *Energy*. Westport, CN: Greenwood Press, 2009.

Everett, Melissa. *Making a Living While Making a Difference: Conscious Careers for an Era of Interdependence*. Revised ed. Gabriola Island, BC, Canada: New Society Publishers, 2007.

Hunter, Malcolm L., Jr., et al. *Saving the Earth as a Career: Advice on Becoming a Conservation Professional*. Malden, MA: Blackwell Publishing, 2007.

Inslee, Jay, and Bracken Hendricks. *Apollo's Fire: Igniting America's Clean-Energy Economy*. Washington, DC: Island Press, 2008.

Jones, Van. *The Green Collar Economy: How One Solution Can Fix Our Two Biggest Problems*. New York, NY: HarperOne, 2008.

Kirk, Amanda. *Field Guide to Finding a New Career in Outdoor Careers: An All-in-One Guide to Navigating Toward a New Career*. New York, NY: Ferguson Publishing Company, 2009.

MacKay, David J. C. *Sustainable Energy—Without the Hot Air*. Cambridge, England: UIT Cambridge Ltd., 2009.

Marquardt, Frank. *Green Careers*. San Francisco, CA: Wetfeet, 2008.

Miller, Louise. *Careers for Nature Lovers and Other Outdoor Types*. Third ed. New York, NY: McGraw Hill, 2008.

Parks, Barbara, and Jodi Helmer. *The Complete Idiot's Guide to Green Careers*. Indianapolis, IN: Alpha Books, 2009.

Pernick, Ron, and Clint Wilder. *The Clean Tech Revolution: Discover the Top Trends, Technologies, and Companies to Watch*. New York, NY: Collins Business, 2008.

Taylor, Allan, and James Robert Parish. *Career Opportunities in the Energy Industry*. New York, NY: Checkmark Books, 2008.

Bibliography

Blodgett, Leslie, and Kara Slack, eds. *Geothermal 101: Basics of Geothermal Energy Production and Use.* Washington, DC: Geothermal Energy Association, 2009.

Bureau of Labor Statistics. *Occupational Outlook Handbook, 2008–09 Edition.* U.S. Department of Labor. Retrieved April 1, 2009 (http://www.bls.gov/oco).

Environmental Careers Organization. *The Eco Guide to Careers That Make a Difference: Environmental Work for a Sustainable World.* Washington, DC: Island Press, 2004.

Fasulo, Mike, and Paul Walker. *Careers in the Environment.* New York, NY: McGraw-Hill, 2007.

First Solar. *Lowering the Cost of Solar Electricity.* Retrieved March 2009 (http://www.firstsolar.com).

Friedman, Thomas L. *Hot, Flat, and Crowded: Why We Need a Green Revolution—and How It Can Renew America.* New York, NY: Farrar, Straus and Giroux, 2008.

Goldstein, David B. *Saving Energy, Growing Jobs: How Environmental Protection Promotes Economic Growth, Profitability, Innovation, and Competition.* Berkeley, CA: Bay Tree Publishing, 2007.

Greenland, Paul R., and AnnaMarie L. Sheldon. *Career Opportunities in Conservation and the Environment.* New York, NY: Checkmark Books, 2008.

Hendricks, Bracken. *Wired for Progress: Building a National Clean-Energy Smart Grid.* Washington, DC: Center for American Progress, 2009.

Krupp, Fred, and Miriam Horn. *Earth: The Sequel: The Race to Reinvent Energy and Stop Global Warming.* New York, NY: W. W. Norton & Company, 2008.

Lawrence Berkeley National Laboratory. "Obama Picks Berkeley Lab Director Steve Chu for Energy Secretary." Retrieved March, 2009 (http://www.lbl.gov/Publications/Director/index-Chu.html).

Llewellyn, A. Bronwyn, James P. Hendrix, and K. C. Golden. *GreenJobs: A Guide to Eco-Friendly Employment.* Avon, MA: Adams Media, 2008.

Miller, Peter. "Saving Energy—It Starts at Home." *National Geographic,* March 2009.

Naughton, Keith. "Now We're Cooking with . . . Batteries."*Newsweek,* December 1, 2008.

Sofge, Erik. "New Battery Player Creeps in on Heated Race for Chevy Volt Power." *Popular Mechanics,* April 29, 2008.

Union of Concerned Scientists. "How Hydrokinetic Energy Works." Retrieved March 2009 (http://www.ucsusa.org/clean_energy/technology_and_impacts/energy_technologies/how-hydrokinetic-energy-works.html).

U.S. Department of Energy. "Biomass FAQs." Retrieved March 2009 (http://www1.eere.energy.gov/biomass/biomass_basics_faqs.html).

Windustry. "Learn About Wind Energy: Welcome to Our Wind Basics." Windustry.org. Retrieved March 2009 (http://www.windustry.org/wind-basics/learn-about-wind-energy/learn-about-wind-energy).

Index

About the Author

Corona Brezina has written more than a dozen titles for Rosen Publishing. Several of her previous books have also focused on career possibilities for young adults and environmental issues, including *Careers in Forensics: Medical Examiner* and *In the News: Climate Change*. She lives in Chicago, Illinois.

Photo Credits

Cover (front, back) © www.istockphoto.com/José Luis Gutiérrez; cover (right), pp. 1 (right), 16, 53 David McNew/Getty Images; cover (left), pp. 1 (left), 40 Pat Corkery/NREL; pp. 4–5 © www.istockphoto.com/Olga Pasławska; p. 7 © Charlie Neuman/San Diego Union-Tribune/ZUMA Press; p. 10 John Moore/Getty Images; p. 12 Mike Linenberger/NREL; p. 19 © www.istockphoto.com/Dorota Michalec; pp. 22, 27 Stephen Ausmus/USDA; p. 24 Kathy Eystad/USDA; pp. 29, 36, 42, 55, 60 © AP Images; p. 34 © Jim Prisching/MCT/Landov; p. 44 © Norman Rembarz/Action Press/ZUMA Press; p. 47 Karen Bleier/AFP/Getty Images; p. 50 Stan Honda/AFP/Getty Images; p. 57 Stewart F. House/Fort Worth Star-Telegram/Newscom.com; p. 63 © Rick Eglinton/Toronto Star/ZUMA Press; p. 67 © Jim West/ZUMA Press.

Designer: Sam Zavieh; Photo Researcher: Amy Feinberg